General Care and Maintenance of
Tokay Geckos
and Related Species

Sean McKeown
Jim Zaworski

The Herpetocultural Library®

Advanced
Vivarium
Systems, inc.

10728 Prospect Ave. Suite G
Santee, CA 92071-4558 USA

Library of Congress Cataloging-in Publication Data

McKeown, Sean.
  General care and maintenance of Tokay geckos / Sean
McKeown, Jim Zaworski.
        p.   cm.
  Includes bibliographical references (p.   ) and index.
  ISBN 1–882770–38–2
  1. Tokay geckos as pets. 2. Captive geckos. I. Zaworski, Jim,
1965–   . II. Title.
SF459.G35M385   1996
639.3'95--dc21   96-52062
                                                        CIP

PRINTED AND BOUND IN THE UNITED STATES OF AMERICA.

Cover photography by David Northcott, Nature's Lens.
Design and layout by Michelle Florance.

Contents

Introduction

This book is intended to provide accurate information on the proper care, feeding, and breeding of tokays and related species of geckos.

The interest in gecko lizards by hobbyists in the United States did not begin until the late 1950s when a few of these lizards began appearing in pet shops. Perhaps the first gecko to be seen in any numbers in America was the large, colorful tokay gecko (*Gekko gecko*). Tokays were also usually the only species of gecko that a person might see in a zoo reptile house at the time.

The biggest breakthrough relative to general information about geckos came with the publication of *Living Reptiles of the World* by Karl P. Schmidt and Robert F. Inger in 1957. This book was widely available in most large bookstores throughout the country and was full of color pictures and lots of information about reptiles, family by family, and species by species. For all the young reptile enthusiasts of the late 1950s, this book was the number one item on our 1957 Christmas wish list. For those of us interested in geckos, we rapidly turned the pages of *Living Reptiles of the World* until we reached page 69. On that page began an entire chapter; eight full pages of information about these unique climbing, talking lizards, with photos of several species, including a tokay.

Soon, a few more wild-caught geckos began appearing in pet shops, and in 1966, Ray Pawley's book, *Geckos . . . as Pets*, first appeared; here were 46 pages with text and black and white photos of just gecko lizards. Many of us were hooked.

Although geckos became familiar to many hobbyists and future herpetologists (people who study reptiles and amphibians) in the 1960s, it was not until the 1970s that articles began appearing in regional herpetological society journals about the proper care and nutritional needs of tokays and some of the other gecko lizard species.

For many of us, our first gecko lizard was a tokay. Its large size, colorful appearance, feisty personality, and general hardiness made it an excellent choice.

If you are thinking of purchasing one or more tokay geckos, this book will provide you with the information necessary to properly house, care for, feed, and, if you so desire, breed your unique lizard pet.

The tokay gecko (Gekko gecko) is one of the most beautiful lizards in the world. Its popularity has been hampered by its pugnacious nature, but with regular handling some animals do become relatively tame. As a display animal, a large male tokay gecko is hard to beat. Photo by John Tashjian.

General Information

Lizards as a group first appeared about 195 million years ago in the Mesozoic Era. Using fossil records, scientists have determined that the geckos (Family Gekkonidae) evolved about 50 million years ago. There are approximately 850 species of gecko lizards. Most are found throughout the tropical, semi-desert, and desert regions of the world although a few species also live in temperate areas. New species of geckos are still being discovered by scientists each year, often in remote, exotic parts of the world. Tokay geckos and the approximately 20 other gecko species in the genus *Gekko* belong to the True Geckos (subfamily Gekkoninae). Close to 600 species of True Geckos exist worldwide. The term "gecko" probably comes from the call made by a North African species of gecko, although vocalizations made by the tokay sometimes sounds a little like the word "gecko." The common name "tokay" is actually derived from the noise this large lizard makes.

Tokays and other True Geckos are unique in four different areas: their voice, feet, eyes, and tails. All members of the genus *Gekko* have enlarged toe pads which permit a gecko to climb or rest on virtually any vertical surface. They are even able to cling to a surface as smooth as glass or walk upside down on a ceiling of a house or on the bottom of a horizontal branch. Geckos and their allies are the only lizards capable of true vocalization, and they can make a variety of noises and calls. Unlike many lizards, true geckos, lack moveable eyelids. The eye itself is covered with a transparent spectacle which, with the rest of the outer layer of skin, is shed every few months. The eye of a tokay consists of a vertical series of pinhole openings which enlarge at night for better (more acute) nighttime vision. A tokay's pink tongue is long, broad, and flat and is used to keep the lidless eyes free of dust or moisture. Finally, tokays share with many other lizards the ability to lose part of the tail in response to being grabbed or bitten by a potential predator. This voluntary tail loss is known as autotomy. The tail can be regenerated (regrown) over a period of months.

A tokay gecko should be held with the neck and or head area held loosely between the thumb and index finger. This will prevent a tokay from turning around and biting. Once held in this manner, tokays can easily be examined in the course of selection. The mouth should be carefully inspected for any signs of unusual swelling or infection. Photo by Bill Love.

Ethnoherpetology
(Tokay Geckos & Man)

Tokay geckos commonly live in people's homes within their native range. They often hide behind picture frames, furniture, or in attics during the day. At night, they leave their retreats to forage for food on walls and ceilings.

In tropical Asia, many stories have developed about these large lizards. Schmidt and Inger (1957) mention that boys in Malayan towns will sometimes tie a tokay to a piece of string and lower it from a second story window or rooftop onto the hat of a passerby. When the toe pads and claws touch the hat, both the lizard and the hat are pulled up to the youngster. Schmidt and Inger (1957) further note that to many Malayan people, the tokay gecko is a symbol of good luck. The length of time between a new house being built and the first tokay barking is keenly noted. A tokay's call soon after the birth of a human child is thought to signify a happy life for the infant.

Other local people have related to one of us (McKeown) that in parts of Southeast Asia, it is considered good luck if a tokay barks seven times in a row. Conversely, it is considered bad luck for the family if a tokay ceases to bark or is found dead inside the house. Elsewhere in Southeast Asia, in the Philippines, church bells in many areas ring at 6:00 PM. This is about the general time of the evening that tokays come down off the ceilings of people's homes and crawl toward the floor of the house to pick off cockroaches and other insects. In many rural areas, the tokays are thought to be coming down to "kiss the ground" and to make a short prayer, as local people stop when they hear the church bells and give a short prayer themselves. Another common belief is that when tokays call a lot, it means it is going to rain hard. Still another folk myth is that if a person purposely tries to injure a tokay, it will jump from the ceiling and become affixed to his or her skin. The person may be unable to get it off. Generally, in the Philippines, tokays are appreciated for eating unwanted insects in homes and buildings. People in the various Asian countries in which tokays occur describe their vocalizations slightly differently. In the Philippines, a tokay's most commonly uttered call is sounded out as to'-ko, to'-ko, to'-ko.

Regrettably, in several other Asian countries including China and Vietnam, tokays are often killed and their parts are prepared for use medicinally. Strimple (1996) reports that tokay gecko parts and a powder made from tokays are eaten in the mistaken folk belief that doing so will relieve respiratory-related conditions such as coughs, asthma, and symptoms of tuberculosis. Hopefully, as these areas become more cosmopolitan, these negative practices toward tokays will diminish.

In Hawaii, where tokays have been introduced, some residents have been baffled by the type of animal making the noises they hear. One of us (McKeown) is aware of one such situation in the early 1980s where the call was tape recorded and played by the media to a diverse group of wildlife biologists for identification as to what type of animal they were hearing.

The Tokay Gecko: an Overview

Tokay geckos range from northeastern India and Bang-
ladesh through southern China and Southeast Asia to the
Indonesian Archipelago. In recent times, they have also
been introduced onto the Caribbean island of Martinique,
to Oahu, Hawaii, and to south Florida. Most of the im-
ports to the U.S. pet trade originate in either Thailand or
the Philippines. Virtually all tokays available through pet
shops have been wild-caught.

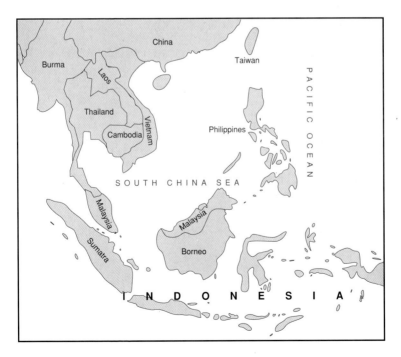

Adult male tokay geckos are impressive in size and color. They are also large and robust with some individuals reaching a length of 12 to 14 inches (30–36 cm). Adult females are smaller and slightly less robust, averaging 8 to 10 inches (20–25 cm). Tokays are also one of the largest living geckos in total length. They are exceeded in size only by one or more species from the South Pacific island of New Caledonia. The average weight for an adult tokay is 5 to 7 ounces (150–200 g) with 11.5 ounces (300 g) representing a truly large, full-grown male. Hatchlings are 3.5 to 4.0 inches (9–10 cm) in total length with a snout/vent length (SVL) of 2 inches (5 cm). These geckos are hearty feeders. Once established in captivity, they are capable of growing to breeding size in 9 to 12 months, although male tokays may take close to 2 years to reach their maximum growth.

In captivity, when properly cared for, tokays have proven to be long-lived. The Columbus, Ohio Zoo Reptile Department under the direction of Mike Goode, maintained one tokay gecko for over 23 years. The Brookfield Zoo reptile department in Chicago, Illinois, under the direction of reptile curator and gecko expert Ray Pawley, obtained a tokay as a wild-caught adult which remained alive and in good health in the collection for over 20 years. The authors have personally kept wild-caught specimens purchased in pet shops for over 10 years, and one pair from these groups is still breeding. So, if all goes well and the information in this book is utilized, your tokay geckos can be pets that will rival pet dogs and cats for longevity.

Selecting Your Tokay Gecko

Since tokay geckos in the pet trade are wild-caught specimens imported from Southeast Asia, the chance that they
will have an illness or injury is greatly increased. It is
important to observe the apparent health of the lizard(s)
you are considering purchasing. Sickly looking animals
are not a good choice as usually they will quickly die from
the stress they have already been exposed to.

First, look at a group of tokay geckos or at an individual
specimen that has caught your eye. Healthy lizards tend
to be active (or reactive, in the case of a tokay gecko). The
eyes should not be sunken in and the lizard should appear
alert and mobile. Don't allow the salesperson to rush you.
Take some time to observe an animal you are interested
in. Observe how it rests. A healthy tokay gecko will rest
vertically on an enclosure wall, either facing up or down.
It will not be resting on the enclosure floor. Also, observe
how it moves around the enclosure. Be sure it is not
dragging a limb or does not appear to have other difficul-
ties in getting around. Next, when its mouth is open, look
closely to see if it has a ball of mucus or excessive fluid in
its throat. Also look for bubbly fluid protruding from its
nostrils. Either such condition would indicate that the
lizard probably has an advanced pneumonia-like respiratory disease from which it is unlikely to recover, even with
expensive veterinary treatment. If there is a group of
tokays in the same enclosure, try to observe all of them in

a general way. If several appear to be sick looking, be aware that the others have probably been exposed to the same bacterial or viral disease, or intestinal parasites that the sickly looking lizards are suffering from. In most cases, a tokay gecko in poor health will be thin and will have a very dark background color with little or no bright orange or red showing. It may also have visible wounds, sores, abscesses, or lumps on the body. An original tail should not be kinked. Regenerated or partially regenerated (replacement) tails are common and nothing to worry about.

Once you have decided on a particular animal, you should ask permission to handle it (at your own risk). Since tokay geckos will respond by trying to bite and can inflict a painful one, caution and good sense must be used when handling them. Handling with a medium-weight pair of gloves will easily solve this problem. If you do not have gloves with you, cover the lizard's head with a cloth, thus restricting the lizard's ability to see your hand approach. Grasp the lizard's body firmly but gently behind the head. This will allow handling without getting bitten. A healthy tokay gecko feels relatively heavy for its size when held in the hand. The lizard should demonstrate a high level of muscular vigor when being held. A healthy tokay gecko should have a rounded tail that shows some fat reserve and gives an impression of fullness. Another healthy sign is good weight around the hip area. If the pelvic bones protrude out then the animal may be malnourished or possibly diseased. A protruding backbone, hip bones, and ribs are very noticeable in many specimens in poor health. You should avoid choosing such animals as it is unlikely they will recover, even with proper care.

When large numbers of wild-caught lizards are being shipped together, overcrowding may result in fighting, leading to injury. Tails, limbs, feet, and digits can be easily damaged. Examine limbs, feet, and toes carefully for unusual swellings, extensive damage or limpness. Check the body for skin rips on both the back and belly (dorsal and ventral surfaces). Look at the vent (the area around the cloacal slit) to make sure there is no smeared feces, indicating diarrhea which would be a sign of disease or a heavy internal parasite load. Examine the sides of the torso for depressed areas or projections indicating broken ribs.

Examine the lizard's head at a distance not too close to your face. The tokay's head should have no major wounds, lumps, or swellings. The mouth will probably be open, making the next part of the inspection easy to accomplish. The normal color of the inside lining of a tokay gecko's mouth is black, with the tongue a pinkish-red color. There should be no white lumpy areas inside the mouth or along the gum line. While looking inside the mouth, make sure there is no bubbly mucus or balls of mucus, which is a reliable indicator of severe respiratory infection. The eyes should have no cloudiness. Look closely to make sure there are no mites between the scales around the rim of the eyes and elsewhere on the head and body.

In a healthy tokay gecko, the anal scales are flush with the body. There should be no swelling of the vent area and no caking of dried fecal matter. As a rule, newly purchased tokays should be checked for internal parasites and treated accordingly. Photo by Philippe de Vosjoli.

Quarantine & Acclimation

The purpose of quarantine is to prevent any contagious disease from spreading to your established collection of reptiles and amphibians from newly acquired specimens. A wild-collected, imported tokay gecko quite possibly could be infested with a number of intestinal or external parasites or could have a bacterial or viral disease. Stressful conditions, which these lizards are exposed to during capture and initial confinement, may act to suppress their immune systems allowing a greater susceptibility to disease and a build-up of internal parasites. You never want to introduce a newly acquired reptile into an established reptile collection without first quarantining the new animal. Quarantining is especially critical when the newly acquired specimen is wild-caught.

Set the new gecko up in a quarantine situation as soon as you bring it into your home. It will need to be kept in a room that is separate from the one that houses your other reptiles. The quarantine enclosure should be simple and be able to be easily monitored, cleaned, and disinfected. The quarantine enclosure should have a secure lid to be escape-proof. It should also offer heat gradients (a range of temperatures) between 78 and 86°F (26 and 30°C), a water dish, and a shelter area for the lizard to hide in or under. Newspaper is the best ground medium (substrate) during quarantine. The materials and tools used for cleaning should be utilized only on that cage. After use, the tools should be dipped in disinfectant such as should be dipped in disinfectant such as Unicide® or a 5% bleach solution for 20 minutes and then rinsed with water. Food items, rocks, logs, other cage furniture, and water bowls must never be transferred from one cage to another.

One of the first things to do upon acquisition of your lizard is to get an accurate weight on it. By doing so, you can determine if the lizard is sickly or not feeding as evidenced by low weight or a future loss of weight. If you have a number of reptiles, a gram scale will prove an excellent investment for quality maintenance of your collection and for providing important information to your reptile veterinarian.

However, a real dilemma occurs for an owner of an inexpensively purchased lizard like a tokay, relative to using a reptile veterinarian. For those that are financially able, an exam or at least a very fresh fecal sample can be taken to a veterinarian. However, it is critical to find the right type of vet. For the veterinarian to be in any way useful, he/she must be an "exotic animal veterinarian" who regularly treats reptiles in his or her practice. Be aware that a typical dog/cat, horse/cow veterinarian will really not be of any help and could improperly diagnose and treat your lizard. Often, if you call a nearby zoo that has a reptile house, they can provide the name or names of a vet in your area that could be useful. The next problem is the cost of the work. Typically, if worming is needed, two office visits are involved plus the cost of any tests and the medication itself. That is just one reason why it is so important to select a healthy lizard to begin with.

Many, perhaps even most, wild-caught tokay geckos from Southeast Asia are going to have internal parasites such as small- to medium-size worms known as strongyloid nematodes. These are sometimes simply called strongyles. These strongyles feed mainly on the blood of the host lizard. This may lead to hemorrhage, ulceration or gastro-intestinal obstruction, and death.

13

It is important to have an accurate weight on the lizard. This can be obtained by putting the lizard in a pillow case and weighing it on a gram scale. After weighing the gecko, weigh just the bag without the lizard and subtract the weight of the bag. Panacur® (fenbendazole) is the drug of choice for strongyles and if you know the weight of your lizard, some vets will provide the medication diluted to the appropriate milligrams per kilogram. An alternative is to purchase a product available through some reptile suppliers and pet shops called Evict® which is also a strongyle medication. The correct dosage for the weight of the lizard is critical and either medication is given twice, 10 to 14 days apart.

A simple setup for quarantining tokay geckos. Paper is used as a substrate to allow monitoring of the status of the feces. Runny or bloody feces are a sign of possible gastroenteritis, and a fecal exam should be performed by a qualified veterinarian to determine the cause and best course of treatment. Photo by Philippe de Vosjoli.

Initially, don't handle the tokay gecko any more than is absolutely necessary. Observe whether it is showing signs of adapting to captivity (feeding, gaining weight, vigorous when active). Offer food in the evening. The lizard may or may not feed in front of you. If it does not, leave the insects in the enclosure and carefully check the enclosure the next morning to determine if the prey items were eaten.

The quarantine period should last from 4 to 8 weeks, depending on the health of the gecko(s) at the beginning and end of quarantine. Also, remember your own hygiene. Use disposable latex gloves, available at any pharmacy, when cleaning the enclosure. Always wash your hands with a disinfectant soap such as Betadine® scrub after maintenance. A good maintenance protocol is to work the reptiles in quarantine **after** you have completed the work in your established reptile collection.

Housing Tokay Geckos

Selecting an Enclosure

Standard horizontal format aquariums are not well-suited for arboreal (climbing) lizards such as tokay geckos. Commercially available reptile aquariums that have a vertical format are much more ideal. In the pet shop trade, these are known as high or H models, i.e., A 20-gallon (76-liter) H. A single tokay can be kept in a 15-gallon (57-liter) H tank and a pair of tokays in a 20-gallon (76-liter) H tank. Larger aquaria are suitable for a male and two or three females. Hexagonal tanks also work well. A screen top with a set pin is a must as tokays are excellent climbers and good escape artists. The screen allows for good air-flow into the enclosure.

A portion of the aquarium glass must be covered on the outside. Use either colorful "habitat" paper available at many pet shops or use inexpensive green or yellow paper available at any stationery store. The purpose of covering the back and sides is to provide the secretive nocturnal lizards with a feeling of security which is important to their well being.

If you're creative and enjoy building things, a custom, wood-framed, glass-fronted enclosure will work equally well for these lizards. Some of the most attractive and inexpensive enclosures of this type we've seen are converted old wood cabinet console model televisions. Non-

16

working console TVs are available free or at minimal cost at yard sales. First, remove the actual television, leaving just the beautiful wood cabinet. Add a glass front. Nail or glue in a solid wood piece to the bottom half of the back. The top portion of the back should be able to be opened. It can be framed screening or pegboard with locking bolts or wing nuts at each end. If live plants are included inside the wood-framed enclosure, a 2-foot (61-cm) fluorescent shop light fixture can be secured with screws into the underside of the top.

Custom-built Enclosures
Custom-built enclosures are also available to those desiring them. Naturalistic glass-front enclosures are manufactured by Vivarium Research Group of Boca Raton, Florida. Glass reptile tanks with side-opening doors are available from some herptile dry goods suppliers including Dick Dunn of Creative Habitat Aquaria in La Crescenta, California. Commercially made screened wood-framed enclosures can be obtained from Chaffee Cage Company® in San Luis Obispo, California and Sandmar Enterprises® in El Cajon, California.

Ground Medium (Substrate) and Plant Selection
Pea gravel or orchid bark make a suitable ground medium for either type of enclosure. Sturdy 1- to 5-gallon (5- to 20-liter) potted plants, such as snake plant or mother-in law's tongue (*Sansevieria*) provide ideal hiding and resting areas for the tokays.

If a glass terrarium is used, a naturalistic vivarium can be created by adding a 1-inch (2.5-cm) layer of small pebbles for drainage, a 1 ½-inch (3.8-cm) middle layer of sandy potting mix (²/₃ peat-based potting soil with ¹/₃ clean sand), and a top layer of pea gravel or orchid bark. Since the tokays are relatively large and arboreal, plants will do best if they are maintained in 1- to 5-gallon (5- to 20-liter) plastic pots which the lizards will also use to crawl on.

17

Setting up a tokay vivarium: A Virtual Nature 2000 vivarium by Vivarium Research Group, Inc. of Boca Raton Florida was selected because of its special features including front-opening doors, screened top, and watertight base specially designed for use as naturalistic vivaria. A layer of medium grade orchid bark was placed as a substrate. This medium works well with most tropical forest geckos. Photo by Philippe de Vosjoli.

Additional Landscaping and Shelters

Large, vertical pieces of cork bark or other tree bark secured in a fixed position, vertical stocks of thick (timber) bamboo, or large pieces of driftwood, are ideal for climbing or hiding areas. Remember, tokays typically prefer to only come to the ground to take food or to drink, so the higher and more vertical the cage furniture, the more it will be used. Be sure to leave open areas between the pieces of wood or bark so the enclosure does not look cluttered.

Another quick and easy landscaping technique is to use several 8- to10-inch (20- to 25-cm) high clay flower pots. Knock a 1 ½ - 2-inch (3.8- to 5.1-cm) hole in one side, near the bottom. Use fine sandpaper to make the hole edges smooth. Place the flower pots upside down in the enclosure. They make ideal hiding and climbing areas for the lizards.

Relative Humidity

Unlike for many small and mid-sized types of tropical geckos, the humidity level for tokays is not critical. A range of 40 to 80% humidity seems to work well. A 4- to 6-inch (10- to 15-cm) diameter, shallow water dish should be in the floor of the enclosure. Additionally, each lizard can be misted once daily. The substrate should also be watered when it has dried out. When a tokay appears ready to shed, its outer skin becomes dull and may be loose in places. At this time, twice daily misting with a soft spray of lukewarm water on the gecko preparing to shed is advised to ensure a good shed. If poor sheddings routinely occur, the air humidity may be too low. The humidity in the enclosure can be easily increased by putting a 6 or 8-inch (15- or 20-cm) wide, 1 inch (2.5 cm) high clay saucer (sold in nurseries) on the floor of the enclosure. Add about ½ inch (1.3-cm) of water and include round

Snake plants (Sansevieria trifasciata laurenti) *were chosen as background plants as well as a small* Ficus lyrata *because the leaves are tough and likely to withstand activity by tokay geckos. Sections of cork bark and dried wood were placed as shelters and to conceal the plastic pots.* Pothos (Epripremnum aureum) *was added to balance out the composition. Photo by Philippe de Vosjoli.*

stones above the level of the water for insect prey to escape becoming trapped inside and drowning.

Vivarium Maintenance

A regular schedule is necessary to maintain an attractive environment and provide a healthy place for the lizards to live. Feces (droppings) needs to be removed on a daily basis. Feces may be removed from the glass sides of the vivarium using a moist paper towel. Feces on the ground can be removed with the aid of a long-handled plastic or metal scoop which can be purchased at your local hardware or garden store. Besides detracting from the beauty of the enclosure, a buildup of feces can present health problems to the lizards by promoting the potential increase of internal parasites, their eggs, or other pathogens. Natural substrates such as earth or gravel in the enclosure should be replaced every 2 to 3 months as part of this preventative health strategy. If newspaper is used, it should be replaced on a weekly basis.

Lighting

One of the advantages of keeping a nocturnal gecko species such as the tokay, is that full-spectrum lighting or other special lighting is not required.

Temperature Regime in the Enclosure

There is considerable flexibility when maintaining tokay geckos. Daytime temperatures in the enclosure within the range of 75 to 86°F (24–30°C) and nighttime temperatures of 65 to 78°F (18–26°C) are ideal. If heat is to be supplemented in the enclosure, a screw-in, low-wattage (25- to 75-watt), red, incandescent bulb will work well. Alternatively, a 60-watt ceramic heat emitter, available through reptile products suppliers or herp-oriented pet shops, may also be used with excellent results. Remember, do **not** use a hot rock with these or other climbing lizards. Inexpensive thermometers that stick to the side of the glass are okay for measuring temperatures in tokay gecko enclo-

A) Red incandescent bulbs are available in different wattages. They're a good way to provide heat for nocturnal species of geckos. B) Reflector-type fixtures are a useful way to provide a basking site for climbing geckos. C) Daytime lighting should be set on a timer to provide the right day/night cycle for nocturnal geckos. Photos by Philippe de Vosjoli.

sures. If you have a large lizard collection, the digital readout thermometer with a remote temperature probe, available at your local Radio Shack or similar electronics store, is a good investment.

For those who live in climates with cold winters, a space heater for keeping their animal room warm in the winter is a must. Most people use electric heaters with built-in thermostats to do the job. Sometimes these thermostats become stuck or their contacts become dirty. This causes the heater to either run constantly or to shut down so the heater doesn't run at all. Either scenario may kill your lizards. There is a thermostat specially designed to control space heaters which has proven very reliable and which will prevent overheating if used properly. The thermostat is manufactured by Desa® International and can be found at most home improvement centers like Furrow's or Home Depot. There are also digital thermometers which have built-in temperature alarms for when the space heater fails. For those that can afford the deluxe Helix Controls® thermostat, one can purchase an add-on alarm that goes off at predetermined temperatures, both at the high and low ranges.

Patterns of Behavior in Captivity

In general, male tokay geckos are very territorial and will fight each other, especially if a female is present in the enclosure. This fighting is vigorous and will lead to severe injury or death to at least one of the combatants. Therefore, do not house males together. The only instance when males will not fight each other is when they are housed in great numbers by importers, and they are too stressed and are unable to pick an opponent from the multitudes of animals around them.

Female tokay geckos housed together in appropriate enclosures will not typically fight each other, although it has been reported that aggression may occur if one female has just laid a clutch of eggs and another female is intent on cannibalizing the eggs. This can be avoided by providing suitable egg-laying sites whereby the egg-laying female can easily lay her eggs in a secure area and by supplementing calcium on their regular food.

Male tokay geckos are normally quite compatible with females as long as each is introduced into the same enclosure at the same time. The authors highly recommend that if new pairs are to be introduced to each other that either the male be introduced into the female's cage or that both animals be put into an enclosure which neither have been in before.

Water Quality

If you are not certain about the amount of chlorine and toxins in tap water in your area, bottled drinking water can be used in the lizard's water bowl. When misting lizards and plants, purified water, which is very low in dissolved minerals, is ideal. Purified water does not leave mineral deposits on the glass which tend to obscure visibility into the enclosure.

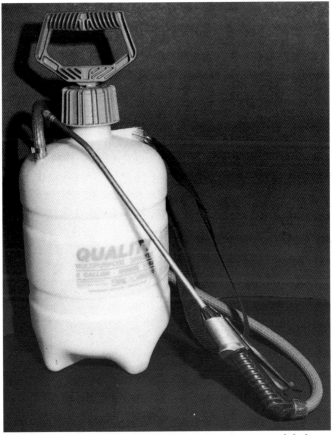

Misting every evening with some kind of hand sprayer is recommended when keeping tokay geckos. Purified water should be used to minimize mineral stains on the glass. Photo by Philippe de Vosjoli.

Feeding

If your tokay gecko has a large enough enclosure with
secure, elevated hiding places, so that it is not stressed,
feeding should not be a problem. Offer live food three
times a week. Adult tokay geckos will take commercially
available crickets as well as cockroaches, moths, edible
caterpillars, grasshoppers, and many other insects. They
can also be offered pinkie (newborn to 1-week-old) mice
for one of their weekly feedings, if these are available.
Mealworms or giant mealworms are not good as a main-
stay and should only be offered as a component of a
varied diet. Presenting food items in the evening is
recommended.

Hatchling and juvenile tokay geckos should be fed every
other day. The insects should be smaller in size. Most will
readily take 2- to 4-week-old (2nd to 4th stage) commer-

Feeder insects should be lightly coated with a vitamin/ mineral mix about twice a week. Photo by Philippe de Vosjoli.

A mix consisting of one part vitamin/mineral supplement and three parts calcium carbonate should be used to coat feeder insects twice a week with juveniles and once a week with adults. If the amount of vitamin D_3 and calcium is increased along with the feeding regimen, the reproduction rate will increase, but in the long run this can shorten the lifespan of your animals. As a rule, it is best to use this higher D_3/calcium regimen with females during a limited breeding period. Photo by Philippe de Vosjoli.

cially raised crickets and other suitable sized, relatively soft-bodied insects. Each lizard should eat about four to six insects at a feeding.

Maintenance of Feeder Crickets in Colonies
Keep crickets dry, offer a slice of orange for moisture and feed oats or high-protein baby flake cereal, or powdered rodent chow. Include leafy garden greens and grated carrots for them as well.

Vitamin/Mineral Supplementation
Prior to feeding them out to the lizards, the insects should be put in a clear plastic jar or clear food storage bag and dusted with a mix consisting of three parts calcium carbonate powder and one part vitamin/mineral supplement such as Herptivite,® Reptivite,® Super Preen,® or Vionate.® Several products made specifically for reptiles and available at your pet shop or reptile dry goods supplier will work fine. When not using the vitamin/mineral supplement, keep the container lid securely on and place the container in a cupboard, so the ingredients do not become stale or unnecessarily break down.

The Tokay Gecko as a Pet

A tokay gecko, because of its aggressive response to a hand or arm entering its living space, and its extremely hard bite which can easily break the skin, is not a suitable pet for a small child. The bite of this lizard, which has broad jaws and small, but very sharp teeth, is painful. This is especially applicable to large males. If angered or upset, a tokay may lock its jaws and hang on for quite some time. Very few tokays will completely eliminate biting, even if they are regularly handled.

This large female tokay gecko is relatively tame although its mouth is open. Taming a tokay gecko is best achieved with younger animals that are handled regularly. An animal should be well established before any time is spent handling it. Photo by David Northcott.

Your goal should be not to get bitten. First, it is stressful to a tokay to have to repeatedly bite, and an injury to its jaws could even result from such activity. Also, an owner could receive a lacerated finger out of careless handling. A spouse or friend will not be impressed nor think it funny if he or she is bitten.

There are several possible solutions to this problem. The simplest and best is to wear a flexible, medium thickness glove when reaching into the enclosure or doing any handling. This will allow you to handle the lizard in an easy, smooth manner, which will in turn cause the tokay to be more calm. The glove can be kept next to the enclosure. However, if you must handle a tokay without gloves, gently pin the lizard with your hand and, firmly but gently, enclose your fingers around the neck and body. Always gently remove it from any surface so as not to damage its toe pads.

Breeding

Sexing Tokay Geckos
Sex determination is relatively easy. Adult males are generally larger and heavier bodied with larger, wider heads than females. Preanal pores along the lower portion of the ventral surface of each rear leg are larger and much more pronounced in mature males than in females. Also, small cloacal tubercles are visible on the ventral surface in males.

Courtship
Courting will commence almost immediately when a male is introduced to one or more females. Normally, vocalization will occur with the well-known "tukko-tukko" or "tokay" sound preceded by an introductory vocalization which sounds like "gah-gah-gah."

Egg-laying
A female tokay typically lays two (occasionally, one) white eggs. As the eggs leave her cloaca, she shapes each to be spherical (round) with the toe pads of her rear feet. Typically, the eggs are laid against solid surfaces to which the eggs soon adhere as the shell hardens. No attempt should be made to separate the eggs either from the surface area or from each other. The eggs are large (0.71 × 0.79 inches) (18 × 20 mm) and they are often guarded from other tokays by both the female and male parents.

Post-egg-laying Behavior by the Male

One of us (Zaworski) has observed the male exhibiting unusual behavior after the female lays her eggs. The male uses his rear feet to mold the eggs in a unique way, all his own. To the casual observer, the egg shape looks like any typical round, hard-shelled, gecko egg. However, there are subtle ridges on the egg surface which were put there by the male when the eggshell was still relatively soft just after egg-laying by the female. One of us (Zaworski) has also observed the male guarding newly hatched juveniles. Specific mate selection has also been observed where one female is chosen exclusively from a group of females to with which to mate.

Egg Incubation

Tokay geckos typically glue their eggs against a solid surface such as rock, bark, wood, or the walls of a vivarium. Following egg-laying the eggs harden and adhere to each other as well as to the surface with which they make contact. **DO NOT** attempt to remove or separate adhering eggs. If the eggs are adhering to a surface, a section of plastic screening can be loosely placed over the eggs and taped to the surrounding area. An alternative, when the eggs are laid against the sides of a vivarium, is to tape a deli cup, with small holes previously punched in it, over the eggs. The main reasons for protecting the eggs is to reduce accidental damage and to prevent hatchlings from being eaten by adults. Eggs laid loosely under shelters can be removed and incubated artificially. This can be accomplished by placing the eggs on a plastic film canister lid or plastic jar lid. This should be set on an inch (2.5 cm) of slightly moistened vermiculite, in a plastic container, such as a rinsed plastic gelatin container. Small airholes should be punched in the lid before the eggs are moved into it. This container can be placed in a small reptile incubator. These are available through reptile product suppliers (i.e., a Hova-bator® model costs about $60). It is also possible to use a small bulb or heat tape to heat an enclosed area to incubate the eggs. A temperature of 80 to 84°F (27–29°C) is ideal. It should take the eggs 65 to 200 days to hatch if they are fertile. During incubation, the vermiculite may need to be re-moistened from time to time if it completely dries out.

Breeding Records for a Captive Female Tokay Gecko (Zaworski, 1993)				
Oviposition Date (D/M/Y)	Clutch Size	Hatching Date (D/M/Y)	Inc. Period (Days)	Comments
07/04/86	2	11/07/86	95	1 egg infertile
01/05/86	2	30/07/86	90	1 egg infertile
26/05/86	2	13/08/86	79	2 hatchlings
		03/10/86	94	
21/06/86	2	03/09/86	74	2 hatchlings
		02/01/87	134	
01/07/86	1	------------	--------	infertile
02/08/86	2	12/11/86	102	2 hatchlings
		13/11/86	103	
22/08/86	2	06/12/86	112	2 hatchlings
10/09/86	1	21/12/86	94	1 hatchling
30/09/86	2	------------	--------	infertile
19/10/86	2	30/01/87	93	2 hatchlings
		31/01/87	94	
10/11/86	1	23/02/87	105	2 hatchlings
08/12/86	2	------------	--------	infertile
04/01/87	2	------------	--------	infertile
09/02/87	2	------------	--------	infertile
06/03/87	2	------------	--------	infertile
27/03/87	2	05/07/87	100	2 hatchlings
20/04/87	2	27/07/87	98	2 hatchlings
19/05/87	2	------------	--------	embryo death
12/06/87	2	------------	--------	embryo death
05/07/87	2	07/10/87	94	2 hatchlings
01/08/87	1	10/01/88	162	1 hatchling
24/09/87	2	07/03/88	165	2 hatchlings
		27/03/88	185	
24/10/87	2	30/05/88	219	2 hatchlings
18/11/87	2	------------	--------	embryo death
20/12/87	2	------------	--------	embryo death
10/01/88	2	30/03/88	89	2 hatchlings
14/02/88	2	21/05/88	97	1 hatchling
08/03/88	2	04/07/88	118	2 hatchlings
28/03/88	2	------------	--------	infertile
30/03/88-10/10/92		Given a 4-year rest		
10/12/92	2	Fertile and incubating as of 03/03/93		

Care of Offspring

Care of Hatchlings and Juveniles

The hatchlings (neonates) are typically over 4 inches (100 mm) in length. They should be set up in their own separate enclosure away from the parents. A 5-gallon terrarium is ideal for this purpose. Add some cage furniture and a shallow water bowl. Feed smaller insect prey than is fed to adults. Do not put juveniles of significantly different sizes in the same enclosure. Doing so may result in intimidation by the largest toward the smallest. Also, returning juveniles to the parents' enclosure before they are full grown could result in them being killed or eaten.

Tokay gecko hatching from eggs maintained in barely moistened vermiculite. As a rule, tokay geckos lay eggs that adhere to solid surfaces such as bark or the walls of a vivarium. A clear deli cup with holes punched in it can be taped to the surrounding surface so that the eggs are enclosed. This will increase humidity and prevent predation from adults when the babies hatch. Photo by Sean McKeown.

Diseases & Health Problems

Shedding Difficulties

Shedding problems are usually caused by too low a humidity in the enclosure. This problem is discussed in more detail under **Housing Tokay Geckos** and **Relative Humidity**. In addition, if you notice a rounded section of solid shed skin constricting part of an arm, foot, or portion of the tail, immediately mist that portion of the lizard with lukewarm water. Next, catch the lizard and, with a pair of tweezers while misting, gently remove that section of shedding. Failure to do so may result in loss of a finger, foot, or portion of the tail.

Tokay geckos have undivided toe lamellae which, if in good condition, give them an extremely firm grip. It is important that, during shedding, the outer skin on the toes is properly shed. If the outer sheddings on the toe pads are not being shed, repeatedly mist the toe pads and the lizard will probably pull the partially shed skin off with its mouth. If it does not and if you should try to remove it using tweezers, be extremely careful not to grab a section of the actual undersurface of the toe as you can easily rip or severely damage it.

Sand Impaction

This condition can occur by the lizard accidentally ingesting sand and the sand becoming impacted in the gut. This can happen when the gecko grabs a prey item off the ground. It is one of several reasons why fine-grade sand or beach sand should not be used as a substrate for tokays.

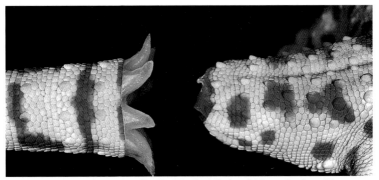

Tail autotomy in a tokay gecko. If grabbed by the tail when frightened, tokays, like many other geckos, will drop their tails. In due time the tail will grow back but may lack the texture of the original tail. Photo by Bill Love.

Lost Tail or Skin Rips

Either of these conditions probably indicates fighting is occurring between several individuals. Immediately pull the most severely injured lizard and set it up in its own separate enclosure. It may be killed if quick appropriate action is not taken.

The lizard that has been removed needs the same good living conditions (warmth, food, and water) as it had in the other enclosure. Any future introduction into the old enclosure will have to be closely monitored.

Burns

A burn spot on a tokay would indicate either that too large a wattage bulb is being used or whatever other heat source you are using is too powerful. Disconnect the likely heat source causing the problem and re-read the information on lighting and heating on pages 20 to 22. Apply Neosporin® to the damaged area on a daily basis. If the condition seems to worsen, contact a reptile veterinarian.

Metabolic Bone Disease

Metabolic bone disease is caused by a diet lacking the proper ratio of calcium to phosphorus and/or vitamin D_3. The most common symptoms include a deformed-appearing, soft, flexible lower jaw, deformation of the limbs and/or a kinked tail. This condition can be stopped and partially corrected by routinely dusting the insect food with a reptile calcium powder of no more than one part phosphorus to two parts calcium, and also dusting with a vitamin/mineral supplement as well. If the condition is advanced, skeletal deformities will remain. Females and juvenile lizards are most susceptible to acquiring metabolic bone disease.

Stomatitis (Mouth Rot)

This condition is uncommon in tokay geckos. When present, it is usually the result of an injury. The first symptoms are reddish areas along the edge of the jaws and a mouth that remains slightly open when the lizard is in a resting position. The infected area may be slightly swollen and white (cheesy-looking) material may be present as well.

Treatment consists of daily using a Q-tip® dipped in hydrogen peroxide or Betadine® to clean the affected area. Afterward, a topical antibiotic such as Neosporin® should be applied. If the condition does not improve in 2 weeks, see a reptile veterinarian as an injectable antibiotic such as Baytril® given in a series over several days may be necessary.

Respiratory Infections

In tokay geckos, these conditions are characterized by fluid coming out of the nostrils or excessive phlegm or mucus in the throat. First, it is necessary to raise the daytime temperature in the enclosure to 85 to 88°F (29–31°C) and the nighttime temperature to 80 to 84°F (27–29°C). If the condition does not greatly improve within a day or two, an immediate trip to your reptile vet for an injectable antibiotic series for the lizard is essential. If you delay, the lizard will probably die. Some vets will show the client how to give the injection and leave the prepared syringe with the client for the remaining injections. This is highly desirable as it may be a real cost savings.

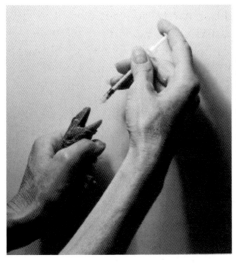

When administering medication orally to a tokay gecko, it should be dropped from above, into the back of the open mouth to prevent a tokay from damaging its teeth and possibly its jaw by biting down on the syringe or tube. Photo by Philippe de Vosjoli.

Diarrhea/Gastroenteritis

Smeared feces around the cloaca, regurgitation, and weight loss are signs of a gastroenteric disease. Call your reptile vet and arrange to take a very fresh stool sample (in a plastic pillbox with the lid on) to the vet for analysis for internal parasites when he/she is in the office. Strongyloid nematodes and flagellates are the most likely cause of this condition. Immediate treatment may be necessary with fenbendazole (Panacur®) for strongyles or metronidazole (Flagyl®) for flagellate protozoans. The enclosure will also need to be cleaned and disinfected and new cage furniture added once the treatment begins.

Mites and Other External Parasites

Tiny mites may be noticed crawling around the eyes or skin of the tokay. External parasites of this nature are acquired at the wholesaler or pet shop and must be eliminated before they spread to your entire collection. This is one of the reasons quarantine is so necessary. Disinfect the quarantine enclosure and all cage furniture. Anything that can't be disinfected should be put in a plastic trash bag which is then tied off and taken directly to the outside

35

trash can. The lizard itself should be placed for 8 hours in a pillowcase into which ½ cup (12 ml) of Seven® garden insect powder, available at nursery stores, has been sprinkled in. Rinse the lizard in lukewarm water afterward, under a faucet. Wash off the lizard's head first so the powder is not ingested (swallowed). Repeat this procedure in 3 days. Be sure the quarantine enclosure is being kept warm and food is routinely being offered.

Marty Capron

Other Related Species in the Pet Trade

Green-eyed Gecko *(Gekko stentor)*

This tropical Asian lizard is very rarely imported anymore, although readers should be aware that patterns of importation can change. It is a large gecko, only slightly smaller than a tokay, but duller in color with grayish-green eyes. Its care requirements are the same as for a tokay.

White-lined Gecko *(Gekko vittatus)*

The white-lined gecko, also sometimes called the skunk gecko in the pet trade because of a white stripe running down the middle of its dorsal surface, is commonly imported into the United States and is inexpensive. It is imported from Indonesia and the Solomon Islands and is a mid-sized species of gecko about 8- to 10-inches (20–25-cm) in total length. It is not aggressive, and its jaws are not strong and powerful like a tokay. White-lined geckos should be housed uncrowded, in pairs, in a 10-gallon (38-liter) terrarium or in groups of one male and two to three females in a 15- to 20-gallon (57- to 76-liter) aquarium. Males can be distinguished from females by their larger femoral pores. When laid on a hard surface, the eggs stick to that surface and must be incubated in situ (in place). If laid on the glass, put a small, clear, hard plastic cover over the eggs. Include a small section of paper towel inside. Make a few small pin holes in the plastic before taping it in place. This is done so the paper can be lightly misted every other day to keep the humidity levels up in the container. The eggs typically take 70 to 80 days to hatch when incubated at 80 to 84°F (27–29°C).

The terrarium should have broad branches and live potted plants for climbing. The humidity in the enclosure needs to be kept high (70–80%) at all times. This can be accomplished through watering the substrate as it dries out and also by misting the lizards with lukewarm water from a spray bottle twice a day. A portion of the screen top can also be covered with a piece of clear Plexiglas® to keep the humidity up. Feed the lizards dusted subadult (3- to 5-week-old) crickets, wax moths or wax moth larvae every other day. Offer three to five insects per lizard.

Although a little more delicate than a tokay, these chocolate brown or reddish-brown colored lizards with a white v-shaped mark on the head and a white middorsal body stripe are very attractive. They make a nice exhibit in a well planted vivarium. These lizards prefer daytime temperatures in the 80 to 85°F (27–30°C) range and night-time temperatures in the 70's°F (19–24°C).

Vietnam Golden Gecko or Yellow-backed Gecko (Gekko ulikovskii)

This species, is just beginning to enter the pet trade in large numbers from Vietnam. It grows to 6- to 7-inches (15-18 cm) in total length. This lizard is a tropical forest gecko, which, in the wild, also sometimes lives on the walls and ceilings in people's homes. At night it becomes active, feeding on a variety of insects. The Vietnam golden gecko is quite hardy like a tokay, but is not aggressive nor does it have the punishing jaws of a tokay. As with the white-lined gecko, specimens will rest on an open hand. Female Vietnam golden geckos are easily distinguished from males in that females lack bright yellow on their dorsal surface and are also slightly smaller in size. Main-

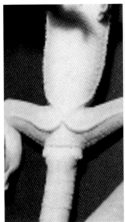

Left: Sexing white-lined geckos (Gekko vittatus). Like tokay geckos, the male white-lined geckos have pronounced preanal and femoral pores. Males also grow larger and have more massive heads. Photo by Philippe de Vosjoli.

Right: Female white-lined geckos have reduced preanal and femoral pores. Photo by Philippe de Vosjoli.

tain this species in a manner outlined for the white-lined gecko. After egg incubation, the hatchlings must be raised in a separate enclosure from the parents.

Gliding Gecko (Ptychozoon kuhlii)

The gliding gecko, sometimes also called the parachute or flying gecko, is also from Southeast Asia. There are five known closely related species of *Ptychozoon*. One of these, *Ptychozoon lionatum,* is also occasionally imported into the United States. While not closely related to members of genus *Gekko*, gliding geckos are from the same general region, are arboreal, nocturnal, and their care is similar to the white-lined gecko and Vietnamese golden gecko, so we have included care information for these lizards here. Gliding geckos are about 6- to 7-inches (15–18 cm) in total length and are gray in color. They have folds of skin along each side of the body and also possess skin webbing between each of the toes. This allows these lizards to escape predators by gliding to another tree or "parachut-ing" to the ground. All members of genus *Ptychozoon* are shy, inoffensive, tropical rain forest geckos. They do not bite hard and may be gently handled. In addition to live plants, include tree limbs with bark on which they will rest and camouflage. Gliding geckos also like to utilize partially hollowed sections of vertically placed thick bamboo. *Ptychzoon kuhlii* can be distinguished most easily from *P. lionatum* by its tail. An original tail on *P. kuhlii* lacks lateral serrations toward its tip.

In captivity, use a topsoil substrate with live plants and keep the humidity high. These lizards feed on third and fourth stage crickets as well as adult wax moths and wax moth larvae. They should be fed on an every other day basis with four to five dusted insects offered per lizard. Gliding geckos prefer daytime enclosure temperatures of 80 to 85°F (27–29°C) and nighttime temperatures in the 65 to 75°F (18–24° C) range. Keep the humidity in the enclosure high (75–90%) by watering the earth substrate, misting twice daily, and having a section of clear Plexiglas® over a portion of the screen top. These geckos can be housed either in pairs or in groups of a single male and two or three females. A gravid (pregnant) female will lay two eggs in a protected location. The eggs take about 65 to 70 days to hatch when incubated at 80 to 84°F (27–29°C). The neonates are 2.0- to 2.2-inches (5.2–5.5 cm) and should be raised individually or in pairs in a 3- to 5-gallon (11- to 19-liter) planted terrarium. They become sexually mature at just under 1 year of age.

Bent-toed Geckos Genus *Cyrtodactylus*

Bent-toed geckos (*Cyrtodactylus*) or bow-fingered geckos, as they are often called in Europe, occasionally appear in the pet shop trade. Lizards of this genus occur in two main geographic areas of the world, Asia Minor (Iran, Iraq, southern portions of the former Soviet Union) and Southeast Asia (Thailand, Malaysia, Vietnam, Indonesia, Burma, and India). Only a few of the Southeast Asian species are sometimes exported, and it is their care and management we will discuss.

The species that occasionally are offered for sale in America and Europe are the Malaysian bent-toed gecko (*Cyrtodactylus pulchellus*), the Thai bent-toed gecko (*C. peguensis*), and a third species, listed on dealer's price lists as *C. angularis*. Male *Cyrtodactylus* are often larger than females. Males can be easily distinguished by their distinct hemipenile bulges and enlarged femoral pores. Depending on which species and which sex the lizards are, individuals can vary in total length between 3 ½ and 10 ½-inches (8.9 and 26.7 cm). Since only relatively small numbers of bent-toed geckos are currently being exported from Southeast Asia and no large-scale captive-breeding currently exists, these lizards are in big demand with herpetoculturists. However, unlike the tokay, their specialized care requirements make them unsuited for the beginning reptile hobbyist.

There are three keys to keeping these *Cyrtodactylus* successfully. First, most specimens arrive in America or Europe with heavy loads of flagellates or other internal parasites. Therefore, they must be initially quarantined, treated, and wormed (see worming instructions for the tokay).

Second, all Southeast Asian *Cyrtodactylus* need very high humidity levels in their enclosures. This can be accomplished by using orchid bark on topsoil for the substrate. Moisten the substrate daily so it just barely dries out by the next day. Also, use live potted plants in the enclosure. Mist the plants and lizards using a spray bottle twice daily. Also, cover a portion of the screen top with clear plastic or Plexiglas® to prevent too much moist air escaping from the enclosure.

Third, it is critical to not keep *Cyrtodactylus* species at too warm a temperature or they will perish. Daytime temperatures of 72 to 79°F (22–26°C) and nighttime temperatures of 65 to 74°F (18–23°C) are ideal. Never let the enclosure air temperature exceed 82°F (28°C) at any time.

INDIVIDUAL SPECIES INFORMATION

Malaysian bent-toed gecko (*Cyrtodactylus pulchellus*)

An upland rain forest species of gecko, it is nocturnal and arboreal. In the wild, it is active at night on trees and can sometimes also be found on village houses. In captivity, include a section of bark for the lizard to hide under and climb on. Feed appropriately sized insects. Maintain this species in pairs. Females typically lay two eggs at a time which are hard-shelled. Incubate eggs as for other geckos in this book.

Thai bent-toed gecko (*Cyrtodactylus peguensis*)

This tropical rainforest lizard is one of the most attractive *Cyrtodactylus* with rich brown body color interspaced with beige lines or reticulations. An original, unregenerated tail is dark brown with off-white banding. This arboreal, nocturnal gecko hides during the day under tree bark or leaf litter and is active at night. Several large branches with rough bark, placed in a semivertical (90°) format are ideal for their nighttime activities. Maintain high enclosure humidity. Feed second and third stage crickets, waxmoth adults and larvae, and occasionally small mealworms that are just freshly shed and white in appearance. House these lizards in pairs. Females lay two hard-shelled eggs which need to be removed and incubated in a separate container. The eggs usually take 67 to 85 days to hatch. This species only grows to about 60% the size of the Malaysian bent-toed gecko.

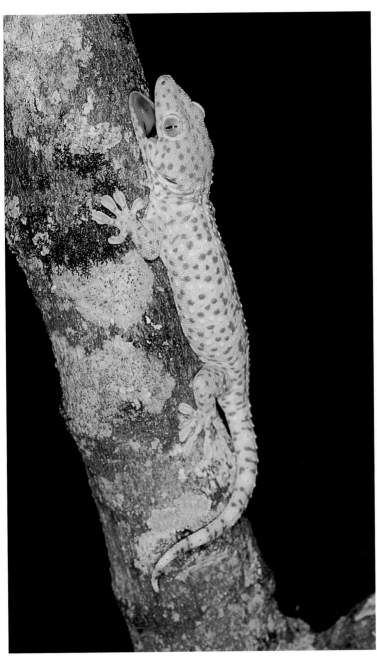

An adult male tokay gecko (Gekko gecko) is one of the most beautiful lizards in the world. Photo by Bill Love.

Close-up of the head of a young adult tokay gecko. Photo by Bill Love.

Female tokay gecko. Full body shot. Photo by Paul Freed.

44

...ite-lined or palm gecko (Gekko vittatus). This attractive species is easily kept and bred. In addition to ...ects it will take fruit baby food or fruit nectars. Photo by John Tashjian.

...rare piebald morph of the white-lined gecko (Gekko vittatus). Photo by Paul Freed.

45

Hatchling tokay gecko. Starting with hatchlings or young animals is a good course if you want to attempt to tame a tokay. Photo by Paul Freed.

Vietnamese golden geckos (Gekko ulikovskii). This pretty species has only recently become available. It is partially frugivorous and will lick nectar or fruit baby food. Some individuals can become quite tame and will take food out of one's hand. Photo by Paul Freed.

ing gecko (Ptychozoon kuhlii). *These forest geckos are still imported in some numbers. Most are hardy captives* *t will breed readily in vivaria when kept in pairs, one pair to an enclosure. Small diurnal anoles and or* Calotes *cies will fare well in vivaria with these geckos. Photo by Sean McKeown.*

ie slightly smaller flying or parachute gecko (Ptychozoon lionatum) *is frequently imported from Thailand.* *oto by Kevin and Sue Hanley.*

47

Cyrtodactylus peguensis. *This small, attractive bent-toed gecko requires moderate heat and around 80% relative humidity to fare well in captivity. It is a nervous species that should not be handled. Photo by John Tashjian.*

Ring-tail bent-toed gecko (Cyrtodactylus louisiadensis). *This Australian form is not usually available in t* *herpetocultural trade. Photo by Bill Love.*

This lizard, sold as the Indonesian morph of the ring-tail bent-toed gecko (Cyrtodactylus louisiadensis), *may prove to be a different species. This form is occasionally offered in the trade. Photo by Paul Freed.*

The giant Madagascar gecko (Homopholus boivini) *and its relatives although not mentioned in this book, can be kept under similar conditions as tokay geckos if kept in single compatible pairs . This impressive species will breed in captivity.*

A basic vivarium setup suitable for most of the species in this book. For bent-toed geckos (Cyrtodactylus), an area of moss would be added. A red incandescent bulb is used in an overhead fixture to provide heat. Fluorescen lighting is used to light the plants and to provide a normal photoperiod. Photo by Philippe de Vosjoli.

A vivarium setup using washed gravel as a substrate with a moss area for bent-toed geckos. The plants are grown hydroponically in containers of water to help raise relative humidity. The gravel surface and moss should be well misted once a day in the early evening. Photo by Philippe de Vosjoli.

Glossary

COMMONLY USED TERMS THAT ARE
APPLICABLE TO MANY GECKOS

Acclimation. The adjustment by an animal to its surroundings when in captivity.

Anterior. Toward the head or forward end of an animal.

Antibiotic. A general term for a drug that will kill or control pathogenic bacteria.

Arboreal. Dwelling in shrubs, trees, or at an elevated location.

Autotomy. Voluntary tail loss; the tail may be regrown.

Bask. To place the body or section of the body in a position directly exposed to the sun.

Calcareous. Consisting of or containing calcium carbonate.

Cloaca. The common chamber in reptiles and amphibians into which the digestive, urinary, and reproductive canals discharge their contents, and which opens to the exterior through the anus.

Clutch. The eggs laid by a single female gecko in one breeding effort.

Courtship. Ritualized behavioral interactions between males and females that precede and accompany mating. This behavior is highly developed in geckos and includes a series of distinctive visual signals or cues. These signals, if successful, include the approach, close contact, ritualized movements, and actual mating.

Crepuscular. Active at twilight periods (dusk or dawn).

Desiccation. The process of drying out. In tokay geckos, this term is most applicable to the eggs which will not hatch if humidity levels become too low.

Display. A specific pattern of behavior involved in communication between animals. It includes any of the senses such as vision, hearing, touch, and smell.

Dorsal. Of or pertaining to the back or upper surface of the body.

Ectoparasite. A parasite that inhabits the outer surface of an organism; e.g., a mite or tick.

Ectothermic. Regulating the body temperature by means of outside sources of heat, such as the sun (= cold blooded).

Family. A taxonomic category ranking below Order and above Genus.

Femoral pores. Small openings, containing a waxlike material, on the underside of the thighs in geckos. These are more pronounced in males.

Fertilization. In geckos, fertilization of one or more eggs occurs inside the female's oviducts, and the embryo achieves some development prior to laying.

Gecko. Members of this large family of lizards are notable for their abilities to vocalize and, in many cases, to climb, even on slick vertical surfaces. Widely distributed in both the Old and New World and on oceanic islands, they are especially diverse in the tropics. Most climbing geckos, such as tokay geckos, have individual rows of scales on the undersides of their toes referred to as setae.

Genus (pl. genera). A taxonomic category above species and below family. In a scientific name, the genus comes first before the species name, and the first letter is always capitalized.

Gestation. The period of development or carrying of embryos by the female of a species within the body.

Gravid. A female bearing eggs or young, ordinarily in the oviducts (= pregnant).

Gregarious. Tending to congregate into groups.

Hemipenis (pl. hemipenes). One of the grooved, paired copulatory organs (double penis), found in lizards and snakes. A male lizard's hemipenes are elongated, rounded pouches which are turned outward during copulation. Only one is used at each mating. When not in use, sheathed in the lateral portions of the ventral area of the tail.

Herpetoculture. The keeping and breeding of reptiles and amphibians in a captive setting.

Herpetoculturist. One who keeps or breeds reptiles and amphibians in a captive setting.

Herpetology. The study of reptiles and amphibians.

Herptile ("Herp"). Any individual reptile or amphibian.

Indigenous. Occurring or living naturally in a particular region or place, but not restricted in distribution to that area.

Interspecific. Occurring between members of different species.
Intraspecific. Occurring within or between members of the same species.

Juvenile. A young, not sexually mature individual, sometimes displaying proportions and coloration which differ from that of the adult.

Labial. Of or pertaining to the upper or lower lip.

Lateral. Of or pertaining to the side.

Neonate. A young animal that has just emerged from its egg, or, in live-bearing reptiles that has just been born.

Nocturnal. Active primarily at night.

Oviparous. Reproducing by means of eggs that hatch outside the body of the female.

Pathogenic. Disease causing. Examples include bacteria and many viruses.

Pectoral. Of or pertaining to the chest.

Pharynx. The portion of the alimentary canal between the cavity of the mouth and the esophagus.

Preanal scales. Scales located on the ventral surface anterior to the anus. In males of some geckos and certain other lizards, these scales may have enlarged pores that secrete a waxlike substance.

Predation. Obtaining food through consumption of prey animals which may be either vertebrates or invertebrates.

Resource partitioning. Referring to the utilization of separate or different portions of the same habitat so as not to compete directly for existing resources. This term may be applied to separate species or to different age groups within a species.

Scale. A thin, flattened platelike structure forming the major part of the surface covering of reptiles and certain other vertebrates.

Scute. Any enlarged scale of a reptile which may also be referred to as a "plate" or "shield."

Sexual dichromatism. Sexually dimorphic in color. Typically, the adult males are the most colorful.

Sexual dimorphism. A difference between males and females of the same species in color, form, or structure.

Snout-vent length. The direct or straight line length of a reptile, amphibian, or other animal as measured from the anterior tip of the snout to the posterior tip of the vent.

Species. A group of animals that naturally interbreeds to produce fertile offspring. Traditionally, the fundamental unit of classification.

Subadult. A young individual that is older and/or larger than a juvenile, but which has not yet achieved full adult size. Subadults may be capable of breeding although, if social, have not as yet obtained a high rank within the group.

Subcaudal. Beneath or on the ventral surface of the tail.

Subspecies. When a population of animals is distributed over a geographic area with diverse environmental conditions, the members of the species in one section of the range may differ slightly in form, color, or behavior from those in another section. Each subdivision is known as a race or subspecies.

Substrate. The material which is used on the bottom of a terrarium, such as soil, newspaper, or bark.

Sympatric. A term applied to two or more populations of animals that occupy the same or overlapping geographical areas.

Taxon (pl. taxa). A specific taxonomic group or entity such as a species or subspecies.

Terrarium. A vivarium without standing water.

Territorial. Defending an area so as to exclude other members of the same species.

Threat display. A social behavior to indicate territorial ownership or aggressive intent. With tokay geckos, this behavior may be directed toward members of the same species or toward other organisms.

Total length. The greatest straight line length of a reptile, amphibian or other animal as measured from the anterior tip of the snout to the posterior tip of the tail.

Vent. The ventral opening of the cloaca which serves as the terminus of both waste discharge and the reproductive canal; in snakes and lizards the vent is considered the division between the body and tail.

Ventral. Of, or pertaining to the underside of the body.

Vertical pupil. A vertically elliptical pupil of the eye that is especially useful to animals active at night, such as tokay geckos.

Vivarium. An enclosure for keeping or raising and observing animals indoors.

Vocalization. Tokay geckos have well-formed vocal cords and a diverse vocal repertoire. Tokay geckos of both sexes are able to make a series of auditory sounds or vocalizations although only the males are capable of making the "tokay" sounding territorial call. Tokay vocalizations vary according to the social situation, such as territorial defense, courtship, and mating. Specific noises are used by both sexes to voice alarm.

Useful Societies

International Gecko Society
      P.O. Box 370423
      San Diego, CA 92137-0423

American Federation of Herpetoculturists (AFH)
      P.O. Box 300067
      Escondido, CA 92030-0067

Literature

Ashton, Ray E. Jr. and Patricia Sawyer Ashton. 1985.
Handbook of Reptiles and Amphibians of Florida. Part Two. Lizards, Turtles and Crocodilians. Windward Publishing, Inc., Miami, FL. pp. 167–168.

Bartlett, R. D. and Patricia P. Bartlett. 1995. *Geckos.* Barron's Educational Series, Inc., Hauppauge, NY.

Conant, Roger and Joseph T. Collins. 1991. *A Field Guide to Reptiles and Amphibians. Eastern and Central North America.* Houghton Mifflin Company, Boston. pp. 84–85.

de Vosjoli, Philippe. 1994. *The Lizard Keeper's Handbook.* Advanced Vivarium Systems, Inc., Lakeside, CA.

Heinkel, Friedrich-Wilhelm and Wolfgang Schmidt. 1995. *Geckoes.* Krieger Publishing Co., Malabar, FL.

McKeown, Sean. 1996. *A Field Guide to Reptiles and Amphibians in the Hawaiian Islands.* Diamond Head Publishing, Inc., Los Osos, CA. pp.90–93.

Pawley, Ray. 1966. *Geckos . . . as Pets.* T.F.H. Books, Jersey City, New Jersey.

Pope, Clifford H. 1955. *The Reptile World.* Alfred A. Knopf. NY., pp. 267–272.

Seufer, Hermann. 1991. *Keeping and Breeding Geckos.* T.F.H. Publications, Inc., Neptune, NJ.

Schmidt, Karl P. and Robert F. Inger. 1957. *Living Reptiles of the World.* Doubleday & Co., Inc., Garden City, NY. pp. 69–76.

Strimple, Pete. 1996. Reptile News and Trivia. *In REPTILES Magazine.* July. p. 102.

Index